Goddess Wears Cowboy Boots

Goddess Wears Cowboy Boots

Katherine Hoerth

Copyright © 2014 Katherine Hoerth
All Rights Reserved

ISBN: 978-0-9915321-1-7
Library of Congress Control Number: 2014948284
Basic Photograph for Front Cover: Karla Morton, "My New Boots"
Photograph of author: Bruno Minkley

Manufactured in the United States

Lamar University Press
Beaumont, Texas

For Bruno

Poetry from Lamar University Press

Alan Berecka, *With Our Baggage*
David Bowles, *Flower, Song, Dance*: Aztec *and Mayan Poetry* (a new translation)
Jerry Bradley, *Crownfeathers and Effifies*
William Virgil Davis, *The Bones*
Jeffrey DeLotto, *Voices Writ in Sand*
Mimi Ferebee, *Wildfires and Atmospheric Memories*
Ken Hada, *Margaritas and Redfish*
Michelle Hartman, *Disenchanted and Disgruntled*
Lynn Hoggard, *Motherland*
Gretchen Johnson, *A Trip Through Downer, Minnesota*
Janet McCann, *The Crone at the Casino*
Erin Murphy, *Ancilla*
Dave Oliphant, *The Pilgrimage, Selected Poems: 1962-2012*
Carol Coffee Reposa, *Underground Mucicians*
Jan Seale, *The Parkinson Poems*
Carol Smallwood, *Water, Earth, Air, Fire, and Picket Fences*

For information on these and other Lamar University Press books go to
www.LamarUniversityPress.Org

Also by Katherine Hoerth:
The Garden Uprooted

ACKNOWLEDGMENTS

I am grateful to the editors of the following journals and anthologies for publishing some of the poems in this book.

Amarillo Bay
BorderSenses
Gulf Coast
Hawai'i Pacific Review
Juventud!
Mezzo Cammin: A Journal of Formalist Poetry by Women
Pantheon Magazine
Raintown Review
The Texas Poetry Calendar
Third Wednesday Journal
Verse Wisconsin

CONTENTS

In the Beginning

I. Her Face Was Lovely Once

Cowgirl
The Venus Refrigerator Magnet
To Catch a Glimpse
Crawdads
The Goddess Scolds Her Lilies
What Sacking Groceries Taught Me
Bloody Knuckles
The Fig Tree
Callisto at the High School Football Game
My Last Game at the Diamond
Asking for the Sting
Carousel Horse
An Empty Parking Lot at Night
After the Flood
The Grieving Sister
The Troop Leader's Daughter
The First Night in El Rancho

II. The Smell of Searching on Her Skin

Demeter Buys Her Girl a Pair of Shoes
A Different Kind of Sweetness
The Last of Idun's Apples
Ashes
Her Mother's Closet
The Queen of Fireballs
Seasons of Gold
Pregnant in Summer
Hailstorm
Flower Picking by Moonlight
On Día de los Reyes
An Enormous Trash Heap Washes Ashore in California
Persephone, Out Past Curfew

Alone
When the Old Mesquite Tree Tumbled Down
For Those Who Search the Peak of Ararat
How a Goddess Drinks a Shiner Bock

III. The Taste of Ocean on Her Tongue

The Goddess Waters Her Plants
A Fisher of Men
Eve Watches Food Network
For Days Like Grass
Winter
Metamorphosis at Waking
Lunes to the Morning
Bird Watching on the Brazos
A Pulga in Alamo
Driving Lessons
Advice from a Maenad
Forecast
After the Stones Fell
Eve at Happy Hour
The Goddess in Her Universe
Bugs
Paula Deen's Paradise Cobbler
Our Tower
Housewife at HEB, Tuesday Afternoon
What Hurricane Dolly Did to My Palm Tree
My Venus Rode the Third Wave

IV. The Woman Even Gods Could Not Resist

The Goddess Destroys
Fall of Girl
Tea Time
Sunflowers
Delilah's Father Takes Her to the Barber Shop
Bluebonnets
A Visit to the Aquarium at Ten
Dulce

Prickly Pear
At Samson's Ford
If Marriage Were a Sitcom
Love Story
Morning Commute
Eve Finally Makes Adam a Sandwich
Goddess on a Lonely Texas Highway
Returning Home
The Funeral
The Grape Vine
Woman, Alone
The Bull Rider

In the Beginning

She made an ocean, ocher, filled with yolks
and gloss, a splash of milk as white as bone,
a sunray stream of butter, clumps of sugar
dissipating into amber swirls.
Then, she sifted what was dry: the dust
of flour, rising up like bits of ash
when poured, a scattering of salt, a drift
of baking powder, altogether formed
a snowy mound she leveled with her spoon.

She poured the flood of batter in the flour,
sprinkled midnight chocolate chips like stars
scattered in a golden, cloudless vault,
spooned her fist-sized worlds onto a pan
and formed them with her hands. When she was done,
she slid them in the oven, licked her sticky
fingers clean and knew that it was good.

I. Her Face Was Lovely Once

Cowgirl
For Io

The story says her face was lovely once
like wildflowers, cheeks a paintbrush hue
with eyes the color of bluebonnet groves.
The story was that her magenta lips
invited in the thunder clap that morphed
her maiden skin to cowhide, ringlet curls
to horns. So now the heifer roams the brush
and snuffs the flames of flowers at the edge

of every country road. The cowgirl dreams
up her reflection as she stomps the buds
beneath her hooves and warns the beautiful
to hide their blooming faces. Petals catch
the wandering eye of clouds, but clouds can kiss,
and sometimes kisses come to sting like flies.

The Venus Refrigerator Magnet

She clasped my perfect math test to the fridge.
Naked, inescapable, she posed
as she had done for many centuries
of men, commanding all to stop and stare.

My mother stood behind me, her back turned.
The sounds of snapping gum, of chopping filled
the kitchen. Echoes of the Cowboy game
rang in the distance with my latest step-dad's
cheers and grunts. But Venus, she was silent

motionless—and I was too, in awe.
Her skin was something I had never seen—
my own was washed with freckles, pimples, scars.

But Venus's was smooth like apple flesh,
her body served up on a scallop shell
like slices ready for the tasting tongue—

a model-sexy pose that offered up
the world her throat. She made me want to trace
my fingertips along her naked hips,
a goddess there to please our every sense.

My mother, noticing I was staring
a little longer than appropriate,
touched my scabbed elbow with her soft, soft hands.

My Katydid, someday you'll be like her,

then smacked my bony butt.

Well, if you're lucky.

She handed me a plate of apples, sliced
and peeled.

Now take that to your step-dad, doll.

To Catch a Glimpse

Anole nestled in the overgrowth
of bougainvillea, among the thorns,

magenta petals, tiny breaths of blooms,
his dewlap puffed out, pomegranate red,

didn't care two kids were hunting him
with butterfly nets frozen in the air.

Raul stared, his eyes obsidian
and wide, a pair of moons.

What's going on?

he whispered in my ear. I dropped my net.
We watched the lizard for a while in awe,

bobbing his head and dancing to a music
we wouldn't hear for many years to come.

That night we left the old abandoned lot,
our mason jars were empty, lizardless.

The streetlights flickered; Raul walked me home
in silence, just our footsteps keeping beat

with early April's first cicada songs
faint, but getting louder by the week.

Once at my door, he asked me what we saw.

I think he's looking for a mate, I said
though really wasn't sure what all that meant.

Let's go back tomorrow, watch again.

He paused, another question in his throat.
Not knowing what to add, I shut the door

and hurried to my bedroom, shed my clothes,
now slopping wet and caked with globs of mud.

I tossed them in a pile on the floor.
The moon shone through my open window,

bathed my sullied skin a brighter hue
of white. I stood there, gazing at the stars

and wondering what anoles did at night.
And there he was, a shadow, just his outline

in the darkness, staring from the street:
Raul. Our eyes met and he froze, a stag

ablaze in headlights, curious, afraid.
I gasped and drew the curtains, snuffed the moon.

He never spoke a word to me again.

Crawdads

I sat along the marsh's bank and watched
my brother and his friends—a ragtag crew

in dirty jeans, work boots and sunburnt skin.
They waded in the shallows, on a quest

to nab a bunch of crawdads in their hands,
and I was made to watch the stupid bucket

where they'd toss their catch. My brother reached
into the water, pulled one out and held

it to the sun, his face in buck-toothed grin.
He ran on to the shore and tossed it in

the bucket with a splash.

>   *Gus, how come I*
can't catch some crawdads too?
>   I asked

and puffed my lower lip, looked up
at him with puppy eyes.

>   *Cuz Dad'll kill*
me if I bring you back with muddy clothes,

he said, then hurried back into the marsh.
I watched the algae part for him and scowled.

The crawdad in the bucket thumped her head
against the plastic wall. I peered inside.

She swam in circles endlessly in daze,
her pinchers pointed up at me.

This isn't fair,

                    I whispered, and then kicked
the bucket over. Water flowed into

the marsh; the crawdad skittered free. I watched
her disappear into the murky deep,

imagining that I could pinch my nose
and take a dive—bare naked save the bow

tied in my hair, the algae on my skin.

The Goddess Scolds Her Lilies

Oh canna lilies, look what you have done!
Your blushing bloom invited over swarms
of dirty old grasshoppers to my yard.
The frenzied come in buzzing clouds that block
the midday sun to nibble off the heads
of daisies, gobble down my phlox in search
of lily breath. They chatter endlessly
in nauseating serenades, and try
to wrap their mandibles around your leaves
as they unfurl in deep maroons. My plague
of pesticide will put an end to this.
I'll watch the bugs embrace your petals, take
their final breaths, then sigh and marvel in
the ugliness such loveliness creates.

What Sacking Groceries Taught Me

On my first day of work I wore a white
t-shirt, red bow tied in my ponytail
to match the logo of the grocery store.
I watched a cashier scan the goods and tried
to sack them just as fast. He looked my age,
sixteen, was tall with bony wrists, the name
Jerry embroidered on his shirt.

First day?

he asked, still staring at the register.

Yes sir.
        He smiled, his braces shone beneath
florescent lights. He scanned a bag of pears,
some toilet paper, then a jumbo box
of Trojans. Blushing pink, he shoved them in
a grocery bag and stared down at his feet
to keep from looking at the man who bought
the things.

A jumbo pack, puhleez!

        I scoffed
and laughed once he had walked away. I heard
footsteps, the heavy clicks of boots on tiles.
I turned and saw the boss—his stomach bulged
over the buckle of his belt.

Hey girl,
you wanna grab lunch after work?

        he asked.
I sneered, snapped gun between my glossy lips.

Uh, no.

      I turned back to Jerry, rolled my eyes.
He bit down on his lip, tried not to grin.
The thunder clapped, and I could hear the rain.

Ok, it's your turn to collect the carts,

the boss said, took a long glance at my chest.

I'll do it,

      Jerry offered, but the boss
just shook his head and grinned.

                  She needs to learn,

he whistled as he walked away. Outside,
I pushed the carts as told. The rain poured down.
I sloshed in puddles, t-shirt, damp and white,
stuck to my skin. The boss was watching me
so I assumed the stance of banished Eve—
a downturned gaze, a pair of rosy cheeks,
my free arm laid across my chest to hide
the shameful nakedness that's underneath,
wet ponytail drooped against my nape.

Bloody Knuckles

He holds his rosy knuckles out, fist clenched,
a flagellant that braces for the lash.
Then comes the song: the flick of skin, a whir
of air, the hollow clank of bone on bone,
the rush of breath between grit teeth and snarled
lips; a primal grunt escapes his throat.

A chorus rings of *oohs*, a murmuring,
perhaps impressed, perhaps to egg him on.
Another whip, another round of pain
to give, receive, and give again, a ritual
I witness, mesmerized in admiration.

I watch the bloody knuckles weal and rise,
obedient and beautiful in shades
of rose, pink lemonade, communion wine.

A silent prayer to swallow down the sting.
The victor looks me in the eye, a sparkle
just about to slide right down his cheek.
I grin and long to feel the burning welts
ablaze beneath my tender fingertips.

The Fig Tree

It was a solid tree, a place of shade
and quietness, that grew along the edge
of our property. I'd spend the summer
afternoons there, scrape my legs while climbing
up its branches to the highest limb
that'd hold my weight so I could be alone.
Underneath that canopy of green,
creation shook with every move I'd make:
a rustling of foliage, tumbling fruits,
the flapping wings of startled mockingbirds.
The fig tree grew the perfect size for me,
at ten, so I could feel like a god,
when every other place felt far too vast
to fill, like it was built for someone else.
The branches curved against my back, the leaves
reached for the sky to shield my nose from sunburn,
and the figs, within an arm's reach, ripened
deep maroon just for my tongue to taste.

Callisto at the High School Football Game

While brushing shooting star dust from her hair,
Callisto yawns. Orion's such a bore
these days; he's always droning on about
the conquests of his past. He draws his bow
but never fires. She puffs the night sky's clouds
away and peers into the world below:
a football stadium effulged with light.
Callisto leans in for a closer look
and notices a squad of pretty girls
stand on the sidelines, pom-poms in their hands
instead of quivers; bows are tied in hair,
not used for piercing flesh. They look like sprigs
of withy, delicate and colorful
enough to catch the eye. But how they dance!
Callisto holds her breath—imagining
with every aerial their legs will snap
like brittle twigs. The band begins to play,
the tubas growl and the French horns moan,
the crowd comes back to life. A hero scores
a touchdown, spikes the ball to show his strength.
And then, another dance routine begins:
They gather round the smallest girl and lift
her up, a pyramid of loveliness,
of playthings for the gods. She grabs her foot
behind her ponytail, like scorpius
in striking pose. Callisto swipes her paw
and thrusts an asteroid through the sky.
All timeless myths unfold the same it seems;
perhaps next century we'll get it right.

My Last Game at the Diamond

It's only spring yet summer licks the nape
and hovers at the back's small. March's wind

kicks up the dust around our baseball diamond,
makes my eyes sting. Just past second base,

a boy slips off his glove, drops to his knees.
I notice how his brown hair catches sunlight,

how he wears the color like a crown ,
iridescent, gold. I toss the ball

to him, he doesn't flinch.

What gives?

I shout,

smushing clover puffs beneath my shoes,
each step I take ignites the monarch rabble

to the sky, a sea with sorrel waves.
He cups his hands, as if in prayer, then peeks

inside his fingers' gaps, pulls out two precious
wings between his pinching fingertips.

He rubs the two together, holds them up
against the sun before releasing them

into the breeze. They flutter off, almost
alive again. His dirty hand held out

to me, he grins: now just a writhing worm
lays in his palm. He drops it to the grass.

I can't help wonder why he'd tear the wings
off butterflies—to feel the dust between

his fingers, wings' edge soft against the palms,
the smoothness at my mouth.

                              Because I can,

he answers, though I never had to ask.
He kneels into the swaying grass again.

I pick the ball up, turn away and touch
a wisp of auburn hair against my lips.

Asking for the Sting

I wore a red dress, red like firewheel blooms,
like lips, like tongues, like beads of pomegranates
or the juice that dribbles down the cheek
after you take that first bite into fruit.

I smelled of Love Spell, spritzed behind my ear—
a tease of cherry blossom, juicy peach
and orchid flowers, should have known that scents
can ride the humid breeze. My dress was short,

slid past my knee and up my thigh, as white
as calla lily petals just unfurled.
And I was sweating in the August sun,
sitting there outside the library,

my head held high like I was looking for
it, something beyond this, beyond the book,
laying open in my lap with rustling
pages. I was looking for it—asking

the bee to come, the sting, the scarlet welt
my neck wears now, reminds me not to sit
outside alone, to smell of fruit and spring,
to tempt the world, to ask it for the sting.

Carousel Horse

He says the world was once a better place.
Half-drunk on port, we ride the carousel
together, share a horse that time has washed
a duller hue. The past comes over me
like vertigo—the smell of thick cigars
that lingered, always, in my auburn hair,
the eerie music from the carousel.
I'd ride these pastel horses, silent, still
mouthful of reigns, forever smiling bright.

He rests his head against the pole and mumbles
how the ride's lights look like yesterday's
night sky,

>*before this goddamn town grew up.*

Where are the wooden churches, orange groves?
His eyes close and he breathes in deep the smells
of funnel cakes, of sweat, and my perfume.

A time when men were free to just be men.

I lean against him, dazed from spinning, recall
how night was then opaque, could shroud the face.

The ride slows to a halt, our worlds return
to focus—blurs of people, lightning bugs,
carnival rides. He takes my hand in his;
the wood creaks as he helps me off the horse.
I glance back at her open mouth, her silent
rosy tongue. He tilts my face towards his,
the roughness of his hand against my cheek.
We kiss. I keep my mouth shut, bite my tongue
to keep the present silent, beautiful.

An Empty Parking Lot at Night

Suddenly you find yourself alone—
the sky's the color of an eyeball's pit,
too dark for skipping shadows, and the moon
even looks the other way. Your car's
across the parking lot that, by the minute,
looks more and more a forest, every sidewalk
crack a bramble, every sound a howl
and every empty car's a shrub the hungry
might lurk behind. You know the fairy tale—
tonight, you didn't wear your short red dress,
meet strangers' gazes with your eyes, or stop
to smell the moonlit lilies at your feet.
You tongue the rouge off from your lips and palm
the cell phone in your pocket, clutch your purse
to your hip. But dear, there's nothing you can do;
the wolf is always after girls like you.

After the Flood

I walk the shore of Falcon Lake alone
and kick a cloud of dust into the air.
A pair of rusted musket balls unearth
and then a glint of white. A human bone,
is my first thought, just one of countless found
along this lake like chalcedony, rare,
but not enough to steal my breath. I want
to trust that floods can rinse all dirt and leave
the beautiful untouched, but I don't see
how drops of water trickling down a shore
erase the rugged landscape's every scab.

I pick the glinting white up from the earth.
It's just a rock, and moist like skin, the face
is sunbaked warm, and sparkling veins run through
with hues of blush. I toss the jagged stone
over my shoulder, hear a lifeless thump.

I'm not the child of Pyrrah; I'm a girl
the waves of Falcon Lake will soon devour.

The Grieving Sister

The story says that I'm supposed to weep
and eek out tears of amber from my eyes

for him, my sun-scorched brother buried here,
his ruddy hair now ash, his bones like stars

that tumbled to the earth. He was the son,
the jingler of keys, the one who stuck

his elbow out the window of the car
and made it thunder, lead foot on the gas.

A foolish boy, he scaled the levee, lost
control, and scraped the surface of the sky.

I want to feel the wheel beneath my palms,
my burning thighs stuck to the leather seats

of father's mustang, rumbling chariot
of muscle he destroyed. Instead, I grieve

for us, the earthbound ones who never fly.

The Troop Leader's Daughter

Our sticks held just above the quiet flame,
marshmallows turn from white to golden brown.

I sit around the camp fire with the boys
who talk of guts, and how, while hiking through
the woods they found a pigeon's body torn
to pieces in the brush. I plunge my stick
into the pit, marshmallow turns to coal.

The boys burst into laughter, hush their talk
of blood.

    If you were lost, what would you do?

my father asks the troop. They talk of earth,
of footprints, broken twigs and skies like maps.

I clutch my precious lucky rabbit's foot,
dyed red and soft against my sweaty palms.

Which one's the North Star, kid?

                      He asks, his eyes
on me. I shrug and mumble,

                  Dunno,
                    point

my finger to the milky sky at one
of countless specks. A boy scout grabs my arm
and leads my finger toward the Dipper's tail.

Right there,

        he whispers in my ear, his warm
breath tickling my neck. A June bug lands

atop my knee, drunk on our light.

I shriek, the scout lets go my arm and lifts
the clumsy bug with pinching fingertips.

He hurls it to the flame. I watch it burn.

Girl, how will you find your way back home?

The First Night in El Rancho

I. The Goddess Sweeps the Porch

I brave the night, a goddess on my own
back porch. I slip into the humid breeze—
la luna curls, an eyelash, while the stars
of Hercules and Perseus gleam white
and flicker on. I part the sea of dust,
my broom's caress wipes clean the residue
of seasons past: the piles of dirt, the leaves,
the carcasses of roaches. Mountains bow

to me. The last one fades, but in its wake,
tucked in the corner of the porch, a snake
uncoils, slithers towards my trembling feet.
The goddess in me cowers down my throat—
I'm no creator, no destroyer, just
another squealing wuss in cowgirl boots.

II. Damsel in Disgust

A snake curls like a gnarled staff,
her tongue parts red to taste my salty sea
of fear. I call into the night, my voice,
a shrieking high pitched scream, flies across
the brush—*Oh hero, come and rescue me*
from these forsythia eyes, that pair of pips—
I'm nothing but a damsel in disgust.
He thunders out just in the nick of time,

as often heroes do in tales like these.
He frames his body in the doorway, slices
darkness with the his eyes of stone, the porch
light flickering behind him. Slay the beast,
I know he will, it's what a hero does—
and deep inside I feel my tripas coil.

III. My Hero Swings His Shovel at the Snake

My hero swings a shovel at the snake.
I turn away—the clang of steel against
cement rings through my mind. The final hiss
brings forth a river, paints my porch the shade
of martagons. Still coiling at our boots,
the writhing body lies—my hero slings
it to his shoulder, naked in the moonlight.
But from the severed head the yellow eyes

still gaze into my own. A headless snake
keeps venom like a grudge within her fangs;
it's something only earth can swallow down,
the bitterness dissolving with the dust.
That night, I dig a hole, I say a prayer,
and tuck the serpent head beneath the earth.

IV. Goddess of the Brush

Our first night in El Rancho ends with me
tucked under sheets and in my hero's arms.
We sleep in peace, are safe from everything
that lingers just outside these walls, the head
beneath the ground. But in my wild dreams
I roam the monte—boot print the dusty earth
in two steps. Goddess of the brush, I brave
the hidden spines of devils head to run

with moth breath, moonlight eyes, coyote tongue.
When morning comes I'll wake and trace my foot
prints home like forest breadcrumbs, home to where
I'm damsel to a hero's arms. I'm safe
for now from all that creeps outside, but still
I feel the serpent sway within my hips.

II. The Smell of Searching On Her Skin

Demeter Buys her Girl a Pair of Shoes

Her Mary Janes were scuffed and scratched, her big
toe blistered, held too tight inside her shoes.

I took my girl to Payless. It was March.
The world was flowering before our eyes
as it always does this time of year.
The peonies were bounding out of pots,
the clovers bloomed in fuchsia in the cracks
of pavement at our feet, and everywhere
I heard the chirps of birds, a baby pigeon
in the tail of the second S,
standing at the cusp of fledgling-hood.

We hurried in the store. But when I tugged
her in the girls' aisle, pointed at a pair
of brand new buckled shoes, the same, just one
size larger than the ones she wore, my Percy
shook her head, her wheat-hued ponytail
whipped against her cheeks with her defiance.

What choice did I have? I let her go—
felt the air-conditioned breeze of winter
evaporate the sweat our palms had made.

She disappeared into the dark and winding
aisles, stopped to peek inside a box
or two, delighted in the sizes, colors,
styles, all the choices and mistakes
that she would have to learn to make herself.

When she emerged, triumphant, holding out
a box as if a spring bouquet of roses
picked for me, their roots still hanging, clumped
with soil. I gasped: a pair of red stilettos
with a plastic flower on the top,
a woman's shoe, a woman's size and style.

My girl, if you could learn just how it felt
to wear this kind of shoe, to let them carry
you into the world of womanhood,
you might just change your mind. I shook my head,

and pursed my lips, although I knew the day
when she would wear a pair of shoes like that
would come too soon for me to bear. I cringed.

That afternoon, I bought my girl a pair
of wedges, ones that wouldn't bring her tumbling
to the ground. They were her favorite color—
the petals of a daffodil in spring.

A Different Kind of Sweetness

You think he'll let me hold a bunny, dad?

I ask while walking through the fields, my hand
in his. With silent puffs of breath I count
our boot prints, each one stippling fresh snow.
The barn is just ahead—its faded wood
splinters underneath the weight of snow,
of wind, of icicles and passing time.

My neighbor stands outside. I slip my hand
free, run ahead—mind filled with floppy ears,
warm weight of cottontails in my arms.
He greets me with a nod and doesn't ask
the reason why I'd walk a mile, to pluck
a rabbit like a crocus from a field.

I stop dead in my tracks. The cold air hits
my face.

    You like that huh?

                              he asks. I stare
enchanted by a whole new kind of magic—
a doe is laid out at his feet, atop
a mound of blushing snow. Her eyelashes
are elegant in stillness, thick and black.
But it's her throat that has me mesmerized;

the knife's clean slit, a portal to the world
of pomegranates, red and glistening,
split open in the sun. I lick my lips
to taste a different kind of sweetness there.

The Last of Idun's Apples

No one could slice apples like my father—
he'd stand there at the counter, whistling
some tired country song, the slicing sound
of knife through apple flesh all but drowned out.
One afternoon I stood there watching him
on tip-toes so I'd see the magic happen.
Just a simple butter knife, a gala
apple on the plastic cutting board.

I held my breath. He carved it carefully,
a god observing how the lines he made
fell open like a blossom in the spring.
Once done, he offered me a piece, his palm
open, the pallor of the flesh against
his own, alive with roughness, moil, and time.
I took the slice and slipped it in my mouth,
so thin that it dissolved atop my tongue.

Ashes

Some things are done in faith, my mother says
while scooping ashes from the pit that blazed
last night. She lifts her hands up to the sky,
opens her fists. Her fingers clean against
the humid breeze that periwinkles dark
with soot. It leaves a dirty fingerprint
of dust behind, a guilty child's, on red
hibiscus petals.

I don't understand

this life and how it works; leftover grease
and coal will make tomorrow's flowers bloom
but dull the colors of today. Her eyes
close and she waits for flowers to emerge
like boils across the garden's lovely face.

That's how it goes, don't question me, she says
and throws another handful to the wind.
Bare-kneed, I sit in grass; my fingernails
split blades. I try to comprehend this world
as ashes gray her honeysuckle hair.

Her Mother's Closet

The closet doors slid open and a sea
of everything that was my mother washed
ashore: silk scarves that luminesce in moonlit
slivers, waves of cotton skirts and blouses

still until my fingers touch their edges,
a breeze of cigarette smoke and perfume.
Tucked away were dresses big enough
to swim in, every color of the gulf:

slate to turquoise with a slant of sun,
to sepia along the shore and sorrel
at the bay. I stood there at the edge
and peered inside, afraid to wet my toes,

yet curious to know just how it felt
to slip them in the ocean of her heels.

The Queen of Fireballs

Sunflowers, plentiful and high as hips,
were swaying in the August breeze, the blooms
upturned and waiting for someone to come
along, like me, and sweep them in her arms.

I couldn't get enough, tucked flowers in
my flaxen hair and petals in the pockets
of my yellow sundress, heavy bunch
of florets in my arms, their fuzzy stems
were tickling my skin. A pick-up truck,
all black, pulled up, was followed by a cloud
of fumes. A raspy voice called out my name,
face shrouded in darkness of the cab.
I squinted, tried to peer inside. A hand
stuck out the window, stained with grease, a flash
of red orbs clustered in a dirty palm.

The golden flowers cascade to my feet.
I reach to take the fireballs from the hand,
their plastic wrappers prickling my skin.

You want more, little girl? Get in the truck.
As I imagine I'm the fireball queen,
my mother's voice resounds across the street.
I tuck the candies in my pockets, crush
the flowers as I skip away. That night,
I pull them out, my seven orbs of fire.
I bring one to my lips, its sweetness burns
the taste of pomegranate on my tongue.

Seasons of Gold

There was a time when summer meant to lie
without a purpose in the fresh-cut grass,
pluck honeyed globes of grapefruit from the trees,
devour them, lick our sticky fingers clean,
to rush through sprinklers, cool our naked ankles,
when days blurred into nights, to weeks, to months
to seasons spent on porches letting night's
maw swallow us. We'd watch the lightning bugs
illuminate the yard with gold and wonder
what it was that made the world go round.

The warmth of August cools into September.
I realized that days and months make years
that come, abruptly, to a simple end.
That's why the fireflies dance, to live again,
you said, lit up a pilfered cigarette,
then let me taste forever on your lips.

Pregnant in Summer

She tastes the hollow nausea in her throat
and ambles through the parking lot at noon
with swollen ankles, heaving lungs, a belly
so large and round it makes you think of worlds.
Summer rivers from her face to neck,
to chest, to bending with the curvature
of earth, the Nile down her thighs. The fetus
flails into the sponge of her, creates
the Atlas mountains with a heel. She walks
with bent back, one hand at the small, the other
resting somewhere in the underbelly
of the Atlantic, counting down the days
until she'll set this globe down, kiss the forehead
of the sky with her own earthy lips.

Hailstorm

My faith tells me a staff raised skyward calls
a thunderstorm, that even hailstones fall
on arid ground, and if the wind-swept earth
can ripen in the summer, so can we.
The rain is coming soon to ease our drought.
I pull my threadbare gloves off from my hands
and head inside the house. It makes no sense
to toil in storms. I know how this will end;
the morning after scent of showers stick
to skin, unbuttoned seed pods lie about
disheveled flower beds. The garden swells,
but only dandelions and clovers bloom.
I get down on my knees to pull them up.

Flower Picking by Moonlight

Once I heard my mother's tired sigh
and saw the kitchen suddenly go dark,
I slipped into the night. I had to know
how it felt to have the moonlight shine

on my bare shoulders, walk the streets
alone in spring with only shadows watching.
I felt the guinea grass between my toes,
the wind through my loose hair, mosquitos feasting

on my naked legs, and I felt free.
Who knew a flower's face would look so different
underneath the moon? A simple fleabane,
something I would step on in the cracks

of sidewalk, seemed to call my name. Its petals,
ashen in the dark, were arched, a cat's
back, and its center opened skyward,
wide, surprise of gold, erect and eager

for a bee's toe or my fingertip
to brush against its pollen-heavy disk.
I knelt to pick it, closed my eyes, imagined
that the hole it left in dust would open

like a yawn and I would tumble in.

On Día de los Reyes

My afternoon's epiphany is this:
some things will never change. The coffee's brewed
the table's set, and all that's left to do
is slice into the sparkling crust of sugar
on the rosca, pray that someone else
receives that hidden plastic prince of peace.
Because sometimes I really just want cake,
to roll the candied figs across my tongue,
taste cherry on my lips and take a bite
without the guilt, to savor paradise
but have no fear of falling to the ground,
the faith but not the burden it might bring,
I lift my palm when offered up a slice:
I'm sorry, no, I haven't any room.

An Enormous Trash Heap Washes Ashore in California

Throw it away; just throw it all away—

as if the earth could make things disappear.
But late one afternoon it all washed up
again at high-tide on the beach, somewhere
on the northern California coast:

the pair of sweat pants that you wore when nothing
else would fit around your blooming belly,
the packs of onesies, tiny socks, and toys—
the things you bought in premature excitement,
a pair of surgeon's gloves, the cotton hand towels
that she used to wipe her cold hands dry,
so many plastic bags that once held loaves
of bread, your favorite cookies, angel food
and strawberries, a pan of casserole
your worried neighbor brought to cheer you up,
the plastic flower pot that held a seedling,
something you could nurse back into life,
the garden hose you used to water it
for one whole week before you gave up, let
it wither in the heavy Texas sun.

The scientists determined that this flotsam
rode the waves for years, adrift at sea,
then washed up on the shore, the grief too much
for even mother earth to swallow down.

Persephone, Out Past Curfew

The story's almost a cliché, my tale
that everybody tells and tells again.

This time it's you—a moon-eyed teenaged girl
that slips out through her window in the night

to join her wild friends, perhaps a boy
her age or maybe older by a year

or ten. You dance beneath some neon lights
to remakes of the country songs your parents

sang along to. Or you're underneath
some strobes that turn your hair azure, a mask

of darkness covering your giddy smile.
Or maybe you're beneath the stars, an open

fire, cicada songs of summer fill
the air. The details differ but the story

always goes the same: your parents catch
you in the act, a father with a shotgun

or a mother with a face that's twice
as dangerous, her anger rustling

her bathrobe, curlers always in her hair.
And then the tug to bring their daughter back.

But it's too late for you because you dipped
your toes into the night and you're in love

with it. Play innocent and cry:

                              Oh mom
you rescued me!

              while yearning for the night
when you'll return for just another taste.

You scrawled your number on his palm; you shook
the slipper from your foot so he'd find you

again; you swallowed every pomegranate
seed you could before she yanked you home.

Admit it—you're like me. You couldn't wait
to fall so fast from grace it feels like flying.

Alone

Was it loneliness that made us search
horizons, shield our eyes from sun to seek

out traces of each other, colonize
the earth? Was it loneliness that taught

our tongues to speak, to mingle, lash and kiss,
and was it simple loneliness that blew

against the sails of a boat, the wind
that twirls an oak seed from the tree, the need

to see our faces smiling back across
a generation, reflections in an ocean

continents away, the shapes of hipbones
in a mountain, tears in endless glaciers?

Was it loneliness that made us see
our faces in the moon, our stories told

by stars, a god with hands like mine creating
sunrays, spinning planets, carving life?

Do we confuse our loneliness for fate?
And was it loneliness that brought my parents

into one another's paths, to share
a single cigarette and then a lifetime?

Was it loneliness that took my hand
and lead me here, a generation later,

looking in his eyes to find the future?
We talk, our faces lit up by a candle

and the same dull stars, consider going through
life's motions: interlocking fingers, pressing

lips on lips, a tangling of legs.
But always in the morning, emptiness

will greet me just before the day's first kiss
as coldness wakes me, draws me out of bed,

and keeps me always searching the horizon.

When the Old Mesquite Tree Tumbled Down

it ripped the roots of morning glory vines,
laid flat the flower beds you planted, snapped
the fence. At first, the scene was hard to look
at: dying leaves were strewn about the yard,
a birdhouse split in two, the sparrows fled,
left eggshell shards and husks of seeds behind.
In weeks, without the shade the branches brought,
the lawn began to yellow like the pages
of a sun-washed book, gave way to weeds.

The old mesquite tree's falling left a void,
a nothingness that needed to be filled,
a wound that only time can fix with what
it has. The vines of wild snapdragons
speckled the rotting stump with countless blossoms,
every shade the sunset paints the sky
each night to celebrate the end of day.

For Those Who Search the Peak of Ararat

It hurts to hope so hard, to search the peak
of Ararat, knees to the icy ground.
They must have heard, as we have, how the earth's
too old for such a flood, and that an ark

this vast could not be born from just two pairs
of hands, a simple man, his nameless wife.
But men still comb the endless hills of hope
for planks of ancient wood beneath the snow

with perfect carbon date, the bones of beasts
that Noah may have rescued from the flood,
an olive branch's imprint etched in stone.
Like us, they come home empty armed. *We'll try*

again next month, you say. I force a smile.
We'll climb into the snowy sheets and search
our bodies' peaks for miracles beneath
the surfaces of silk, of skin, of flesh.

How a Goddess Drinks a Shiner Bock
Demeter's Advice for Thirsty Women

You must come thirsty—hair wind-tangled, face
sun-burnt, the smell of searching on your skin.
Forget all you've been taught: to sip from flutes
like hummingbirds from jacaranda blooms,
one droplet at a time. A goddess swigs
straight from the bottle. Let your lips touch foam,
let tongue meet bock, let amber rivers flow.
Then close your eyes and dream of spring's return:
mesquite blossoms, ochre, full and tumbling,
yuccas reaching sunward, gold and ripe,
soft grass on calloused feet like lips on lips.

Let eyelids wrinkle; let toes kink, and drink
in gulps until your thirst is satisfied.
Mustached in froth—slide wrist across your mouth.

When mortals laugh, laugh back. Demeter's stare
could fork the tongue of man and shrink him down—
a fire-bellied newt beneath her boots.
A goddess isn't coy; embrace your thirst,
the quenching. Raise your bottle high. Shout *prost*.

III. The Taste of Ocean on Her Tongue

The Goddess Waters her Plants

I tend this garden, ritual as dawn;
I come to bead the thirsty with my hose.

I overlook lantana sprigs that burst
in shades of sunrise at my naked feet.

All florets lean their faces to the sky;
my eyes are no exception, creeping up

toward sunlight like the eager buds of figs.
I see a man, his shoulders broad, his skin

the auburn shade of earth, ascend my palm.
His hands reach up to touch the crown of fronds.

His saw hums like a bee and aged leaves sway.
The skirts fall first and then white flowers drop.

I soften like cenizo leaves, my mouth
hangs open, fuchsia and in bloom. The hose

sprays on and water puddles at my feet.
A toad emerges from the weeds and croaks

as if to thank me for the summer bath.

A Fisher of Men

She didn't cast a net into the waves
or heave it, full and bustling to the shore.
She didn't need a pole, a tackle box
with every lure from flies to plastic worms
to baubles in cerise or copper shades.
Nor did she need a bucket filled with shrimp
and roily water, sun-washed hat, fishhooks
pierced through the visor to commemorate
the thousand gasping lips she'd hooked before.

Only this: the earlobe's subtle curve,
the earthy scent of whisper, tender curl
of tongue to make him nibble, stir beneath
the darkness of the waves, to take a bite.
So she could pull him up into the light
and fill his lungs with air, to make him see
the world was beautiful beneath the sun.
And so begins the story we all know:

Eve Watches Food Network

I've seen them served so many different ways—
a handful hidden in an emerald bed
of fresh arugula, thin slices nestled
on a slick of mascarpone cheese
to top a tart. They're boiled to a sauce
with port, balsamic vinegar and honey,
smashed into a jam and served on toast.
Some slice them open, dig the insides out,
that earthy core, to stuff them full with feta,
wrap them up with festoons of prosciutto.
All this to tempt the hungry, make him bite!

But I remember simply reaching up
plucking a ripe one from the hanging branches.
I told him, *close your eyes, love,* slid the fruit
across his lips. He nibbled, then gave in.
That's when I learned there's nothing sweeter than
the simple succulence of naked figs.

For Days like Grass

As for man, his days are like grass, he flourishes like a flower of the field
      Psalm 103:15

Our days begin like grass and bend
together in a symphony
of even green. Today's the blade
you set the grocery bags atop
the kitchen counter. We unpack
the bounty, not a word between
us: peppers smell of spring, a sack
of lemons yellow like its wane.

We've watched the graft between us loosen
with the skin around my smile,
but I don't weep like hollyhocks
in fall. A carnation bouquet
falls from your hands, crestfallen
flowers lay before our feet.

Winter

The trees rejoice the snow's return,
and leaves of oaks fall to the ground
like satin lingerie. They revel
in the barren twigs that still reach up
for warmth without the crowning green,
the succulence of April fruits.

And though the hyacinth vines that wrapped
around the trucks begin to fade,
perennials like bleeding hearts
will bloom. I breathe the earthly smell

the freeze brings up from dust. At dusk
the crows return to lifeless trees
to roost, reanimate them once
again, effulgent with their violet
shades, their branches now alive
more than before. Everything
is beautiful in spring, but nothing
thrives more than a winter bloom.

Metamorphosis at Waking

Her days begin at dawn when she awakes,
unfurls her arms and stretches out her legs,
colossus of the world built in her dreams
where she is goddess, queen of open seas,
and every wave curls at her toes for her.
Each morning she's reborn, emerges from
the ocean of her sheets full-formed with yawns
like wind and seashell skin awash with salt.
She rubs the fog out from her eyes and slips
into this world, untangling the seaweed
of her hair and washing out the scent
waves and sweat, exchanging it for lilac,
something pleasant. Here, she's made to serve.

She pours herself into her uniform,
a pair of shoes, ties back her wild hair
into a bun and shuffles off to work
where she'll wipe tables, grind your coffee beans
and tie an apron at her back's small, green
and tight around the hips. Nothing lulls
you closer than her siren's voice, asking
how you take your morning cup of joe
through the drive-thru window with a smile,
promising to pour the perfect cup.

Lunes to the Morning

This is you:
a catkin on the branch
about to burst,

waiting for winds
of spring, for hungry bees,
swarms of monarchs

that time brings
to a trickle. The air
is pollen thick,

the heavy clouds
hang above, a periwinkle sky
slips its tongue

into your mouth
and lets the rain fall
on thirsty ground,

the water welcome
only on your parched lips,
dry like Texas.

Bird Watching on the Brazos

I catch a glimpse of ashen feathers slip
into a ripple, hear a quiet splash
against the breakers' chorus, nothing more,
the traces of it swallowed by a wave.
Birds don't disappear, it must be lost—
in this infinity of water, bubbles,
sky. Binoculars fall to my chest;
it's hopeless, waiting for a resurrection.
It's sunset. Countless birds return to roost:

A flock of laughing gulls, so numerous
the tourists cringe, a white crane, ankles damp
with froth from wading in the shallow bay,
a pelican with wings outstretched to catch
the breeze. And then, a beak breaks through
the surface and a cormorant emerges
shaking off the beads of sparking water
from its feathers, rides the waves to catch
her breath. I watch her leap into the air
rejoin the dusky sky, the falling sun.

A Pulga in Alamo

After A Supermarket in California by Allen Ginsberg

What thoughts I had of you
this afternoon, as I strolled

through the stalls of la pulga
in Alamo, thirsty for shade,

 a sip of coke from a glass bottle,
images and inspiration, hoping

for a glimpse of holiness
on the shine of a bruised tomato,

in the penumbras of split papayas.
Who built this shrine to life

where abuelitas barter for cilantro plants
that bound from plastic manteca containers?

Nietos, palms outstretched for dulces
smile and their teeth shine silver.

Babies ride the hips of their mothers
and toddlers grab a tia's hand, scream

with songs of pirated cds, as loud
as a Texas sun. I found Neruda there,

in the nose of the mutt, in the smell
of burning mesquite and carnitas.

Whitman, too, was stroking his beard
in a mixture of bewilderment and awe

at the tiny leaves of grass, the struggle
to survive in spite of all these chancla'd feet.

Where have you wandered off to?
Which way did your lips take you?

Did you taste the aguas frescas yet?
The cantaloupe is sweet, a grocery boy's

kiss in spring. I'll follow the sound
of cumbias to where Charon's ferry

wrecked along the river's muddy banks,
just in time before he met that final destination—

the gulf's frothing mouth of forgetfulness.

Driving Lessons

First, you must let go of destinations,
roads, my girl, don't end, they only wind,
and wind, and wind. Love the driver's seat;
love going anywhere you please, the power

to rest in some forsaken town, or blur
it with your speed if you desire another
hour or two of travel. Learn to love
the steering wheel's vibration on your palms—

try hugging curves, sharp turns, and straight shots west.
Sometimes the body wants an open road
and nothing more. Girl, roll your windows down;
let summer tangle up your hair,

and taste it on your sunburnt lips. You're in
control, so thrust the gas when you want more,
and slam the breaks when you desire less.
Only you can make your engine moan,

your tires squeal, your windshield wipers sing.
Stop only when the body wills it, breathe
the bitter scent of coffee from the Shell
and find a place to rest your head tonight.

Advice from a Maenad

Choose your wine as if it lasts for life
even if, by sunrise, every trace

of it gets swallowed down or stains your lips.
A maenad's led by her desires, knows

exactly what she wants but isn't shy
to gulp from every bottle, from the creamy

chardonnays that slide right down the throat,
the muscular merlots that fill the mouth

with flavor, to the cabernets, austere,
that need your loosening to breathe again.

Pour a glass of everything and roil
it round the rim. Lean in close and take

in the bouquet, the scents of fruit, of earth
the musk of toil. The first sip's like a kiss;

let it past your lips, your tongue, your throat.
Savor tartness in your mouth, the bite,

the way it fills your palette with the promise
of saliva. Send away what fails

to give you pleasure with a laugh, the flabby
ones that fail to pique your buds. Take home

what does, what leaves you sucking on your lips
with anticipation. Toast the setting sun,

uncork the night, and raise a glass to all.
Draw back the curtains, drink until you taste

the earth, the clouds, the rain, the sweat. Drink
until you're satisfied then drink another

glass until there's nothing left to do.
When morning pounds its fists against your windows,

wake with violet lips, a parched throat, heavy
head that fogs with memories of pleasure,

and the subtle aftertaste of shame
that always seems to follow on your breath.

Forecast

The weatherman predicts a hurricane,
and like a seer reading patterns tea

leaves make inside a cup when sipped and swirled,
he asks me to suspend my disbelief,

have faith in something I can't understand.
He gives the warning signs: the barometric

pressure, ocean temperature as warm
as water drawn for baths, and buoys tell

us how the waves are kicking up, the winds
are wrapping round themselves like steam arising

from a cup of coffee. No one's seen
it yet, but just imagine cloud walls thick

like pillars in the sky, a churning storm
lost somewhere in the middle of the gulf

with raindrops warm as breath. He reads the ocean
like a map of stars and says beware—

evacuate and head for higher ground.
For those who choose to stay: board up your windows,

hoard canned goods, bottled water, batteries.
Light your candles, say a prayer, and hope.

After the Stones Fell
For the Freak McAllen Hailstorm, 2012

The storm stripped every blossom
from my grapefruit tree, shredded
them with jagged ice. I had to count
the hundred alabaster stars, strewn
across my lawn, each one an unkept
promise of sugar to the tongue.

I tell myself, have faith. Even violent storms
have sweetness to offer: towers of clouds,
cumulonimbus, are beautiful when laced
with ice; they dribble dulcet rain onto leaves.
Think of water lost in an infinity of sky,
how layer after glistening layer of white
creates a tiny orb, a world of crystal
high above the one beneath my boots.

But this is all beyond my fingertips.
I run my hand across the tree's stippled bark,
touch the twigs' snapped points, bare branches,
recount the fragrant blossoms on the ground.

Come morning, the looming clouds will drift.
The sun will melt the ice, and hailstones
will dissolve into the earth like sugar
melting into the ruby of grapefruit flesh.

Eve at Happy Hour

So this is Eden, almost paradise—
a smoke filled bar, a frozen daiquiri,

and me, sleek hummer in an iridescent
dress, whose come to drink it in, to sip

from every flower with a swizzle straw
and watch before her as the well-known tale

unfolds within the shadows of this place.
Most fruits hang low—the man a few stools down

with too much aftershave, the desperate scent
of peaches past their prime and one who sits

across a table from his wife, his fingers
covering the apple of his throat.

He strokes it like a secret as his eyes,
like mine, gaze upward, past this paradise

as if he knows there's more to life than milk
and honeyed chardonnays. The ones with lips

already stained in mauve taste sweetest now.
I pierce my maraschino with my straw,

remembering my first bite into fruit.

The Goddess in her Universe

I sit amongst it all, in my backyard,
where songs of mockingbirds trill in the distance
while a pair of grackles preen their feathers
for attack. A kudzu vine's embrace

deprives a fledgling palm tree's fronds of sun.
My aloe vera reaches skyward, buds
like fingers of the ravenous for bread.
Lantanas, smothered by their tangled roots

inside a pot that's far too small, are bounding
over the rim in search of fragrant earth.
Hibiscus plants I put into the ground
three springs ago are blushing full of life

to call the swarms of bees into their flowers.
Every year they sag a little lower
with their untouched pollen as the drifts
of honeybees and butterflies grow thin.

Bugs

You have to sweep them underneath the rug,
or chase them back into the crevices
they came from. Colonies of sugar ants
creep in to catch the crumbs too small to see.
A silverfish has deemed my shower drain
his home, and can't you hear the crickets sing
each night? They're not outside. I try to sleep
as moths' heads clink against the chandelier
I left aglow. The daddy long-legs feast
upon the crowds; I brush their webs away
each morning from the kitchen's every nook.

A home is never free from creeping bugs
and it's impossible to kill them all.
To live, sometimes you have to close your eyes,
pretend that everything's ok inside
and make the ugly traces disappear.

I ask about your day or what's for lunch
and not the chaos of what's underneath
that placid face, the thumping of my heart—
a spec of flea dirt in the bed sheet's wrinkle,
the cockroach nestled within the duvet.

Paula Deen's Paradise Cobbler

Are you a whip or spoon girl?
                              Paula asks
into the camera, but I think it's just
to me. I watch her beat a batter, spoon
in hand. She peels the apples, flecks of green
skin sail into the sink and speckle it
with hues of gardens overgrown in spring,
the smooth grass snakes it hides.

                         Don't be afraid
of granny smiths, their tartness won't hurt none.

She dumps the apple flesh into her bowl
of cobbler batter, pops it in the oven
with a dust of cinnamon on top
and smiles. So little our tongues change, it seems.
Today, we need the tangy lips of Eve
to taste the milk and honey of a dish.

Our Tower

We play a game of Jenga
after dinner when
there's still a bit of wine
left in my glass, too much
to swallow in a gulp
or two. This passes time
before we both will tumble
onto one another
in our bed. I watch
him build it up, each game
begins the same, a tall
and sturdy tower full
of hope that this will last
my picking or his shoves,
our clumsy carelessness.
I go first. I pull
a piece out from the bottom—
that's the kind of woman
that I am. He's smart,
though, balances my taking
with his own slick movements,
slides a piece and sets
it on the top. This game
goes on all night it seems.
The moon is rust. I down
my wine, breath deep. The trick
is leaving your opponent
an imbroglio
of blocks when it's his turn.
The truth is that it all
comes down to this: the loser's
just the one that pulled
the final straw. We watch
it totter then we laugh
as all the blocks come crashing,
spilling everything

out on the kitchen table.
Though the one left pointing
her finger wins, the mess
belongs to both of us.

Housewife at HEB, Tuesday Afternoon

I.
The hunger brought her here. It brings us all
to these brick walls, the aisles we wonder through
in search of inspiration. The recipes
she followed had grown stale, the flavors dull,
even good tongues need change. The glass doors part,
a sea of faces and florescent lights.
The cart wheels clank, she pushes through without
hesitation. Cold air on cheeks and sweat
evaporates; the nape is quick to dry.

II.
A babbling of scents from all across
this earth: oregano, cilantro, mint,
and leaves of tarragon amalgamate
and fill the air. The housewife breathes it in
imagining the thousand ways to slice
each herb, meanders through the produce aisle
in search of something more. The fruit comes next,

a bag of stiff, unripened avocados,
papaya cradled in a young girl's arms,
a fist of figs to savor. Grapes in deep
maroon, temptations at the fingertips.
The housewife plucks one, slips it past her lips
in one thrust, swallows down the seed. She leaves
the produce aisle with just a touch of sweetness
on her breath, a bitter aftertaste.

III.
A wet floor sign, the tiles slick, reflect
the endless rows of lights like guiding stars.
She hurries through. The cartwheels splash a stream
of umber droplets on her espadrilles.
Pillar of salt in aisle two, one hundred
girls with white umbrellas in the rain.

The housewife grabs the top container, turns
around the corner, never glances back.
Another item to cross off her list.

IV.
Heaven is the smell of fresh bunuelos.
The baker sets them in the pastry case
and dusts them with a touch of cinnamon.

A child grabs ones, smiles and skips away;
Another pastry slides to take its place,
the never-ending cycle, bread and bread
and flesh and flesh. The housewife hurries through
the bakery, sucks in her stomach, sighs.

V.
The glass doors part without even the flick
of a wrist. It's just another mundane trip
for her, like countless trips before. The heat
of summer greets her once again. She squints
her eyes, ducks out into the Texas sun.

What Hurricane Dolly Did to my Palm Tree

She was a lover of the loose,
could bring a skirt down to the floor
beginning with a gentle sway,
a slow-dance in the dark, two awkward
teenaged girls at prom, unsure
of who should lead and who should follow.
The winds kicked up, the music changed
to cumbias that brought their bodies
close, a finger ran through loose
and tangled hair, a gasp of gusts,
a whistle of the wind, an arm
around the waist and she let go.

I closed my eyes and went inside.
I couldn't watch this dance for fear
that I would too become a willing
victim to the storm, my body
wet with raindrops, open arms
to let her take me to the sky
and sing the songs of hurricanes.

In the moments when the eye
passed over, I crept out again
to find discarded taupe skirts strewn
around the garden bed, my palm
tree standing, naked, breathless, ready
for another dance with Dolly.

My Venus Rode the Third Wave

The story says the wind blew Venus home,
that somewhere in the middle of the sea
she was waiting on her scallop shell
with clean skin, smooth like whorls of baby's ear,
her wisping hair, her patient hazel eyes.
But this is not the Venus I imagine
when I smell the ocean's briny spray
or hear its distant whisper in a whelk.

My Venus felt the salt's sting on her skin
and opened sunray shells with fingertips.
My Venus tasted ocean on her tongue
and licked her lips. My Venus swam through flotsam,
seaweed tangled in her golden hair.
My Venus rocked the ocean, made the waves,
then rode the third one to the coastal bend,
and breathless, heaving, dug her fingernails
into the curves of sandy dunes, with earth
between her naked toes, the froth of waves
sluicing her ankles and her conch shell clean.

IV. The Woman Even Gods Could Not Resist

The Goddess Destroys

If water is the cleanest way
to kill a flea, then open up
the heavens, let their windows crack,

let chips of stained glass bloom across
my lawn like clover puffs. I clutch
the hose and open up the spout.

I smile sinister, the flood
begins. The dust beneath my boots
turns into mud as rivers lift

up acorns long dried out, the husks
cicadas left behind, the still
and lifeless wings of owl moths.

The water eddies, animates
them once again, washes clean
the crannies where the filthy tucked

themselves away from all my wrath.
There's no salvation from these waves,
And I extend no olive branch

to the unclean in my backyard.
I dream of tiny nostrils filled
with rain, the moment when the flea

gives up and sinks down to the ground.
I twist the faucet shut; I snap
my fingers and the rivers halt.

Fall of Girl

While skating down suburban streets,
the hot breeze hit my oily skin.

My teenage mind was cumulus
and filled with boys who played guitar,
drove rusty pickup trucks, or scored
touchdowns beneath the Friday lights.

I sliced into the pavement, turned
the corner, heard a whistle from
behind, and then a voice call out:

Hey pretty gal, slow down, and let
us get a better look at you.

A lady shouldn't turn around
as if all catcalls were for her.
I peeked over my shoulder, saw
behind me there were three young men
with goofy smiles, one wore a wife
beater, another had a 'stache.

Hey pretty gal! How old are you?

His words like hungry fingertips
that test the ripeness of a peach.
I sneered. I turned my back and raised
my fist up to the sky, then stretched
my middle finger high. I thought
their jeers would echo through the street.

Instead, I only heard the lilts
of mockingbirds. A wicked grin
sliced into my guileless face.
I picked up speed and took a turn

too fast. My balance lost, I fell
onto the street and skinned my knees.

But I remember looking back,
relieved to find no one had seen
my nasty fall from grace, relieved
to know the hands of men weren't what
I needed to rise up again.

Tea Time

With specks sawdust in his mullet, beads
of sweat distort the semper fi tattooed
onto his arm, he smelled of musk, of pine,
his voice a rasp from shouting over sawmills.
This is how I learned what made a man
a man: my father, at the kitchen table,
head resting in the leather of his palms,
exhaled the roughness that he wore outside

letting his face fall into gentle smile.
I'd pour a steaming cup of nothing, join
the court of plush toys draped in plastic jewels.
He takes a sip, the tiny teacup lost
in his hands, the porcelain's clank. How seamlessly
he'd slip into this world that couldn't fit—
a world of girls where hands are smooth, where men
are charming, live in castles, save the day.

Sunflowers

They grew like weeds, taller than my legs
at ten, sunflowers by the row along

the schoolyard's edge in early May, the summer
about to open up. I sat alone,

beneath the shade of the pavilion,
licking a push-pop, gingering my tongue,

and watching how the boys would make the burning
yellow blossoms dance while running through

them, fingering the petals, lopping off
the heads, and laughing as the black-eyed centers

tumbled to the dust. I couldn't look away
as one by one they snuffed the flowers out.

The bell rang and they rushed past, smell of sweat
and musk trailed close behind. I stood up, shook

the dust off from my shorts and one boy stopped.
He pulled a flower from his pocket, stem

attached, and held it out, an offering
to me. I took it, smoothed the crumpled petals.

His eyes were two dark flower disks on me
as my clenched fist beheaded it, so sift

and clean it almost took his breath away,
the Adam's apple bobbing in this throat.

Delilah's Father Takes Her to the Barber Shop

My father threw his hands up in defeat.
Perhaps it had become too much for him—
the nightly fight to pull out every snarl,
occasional entangled piece of gum,
or maybe how sometimes I'd hide my eyes
behind that golden lamb's wool veil of hair
whenever I just couldn't face the world.

He took me to the barbershop between
the hardware and liquor stores on Main,
and Frank, same man who shaved my father's head
on Sunday evenings, lifted me into his barber chair
and pumped it towards the sky. I closed my eyes
and felt rough fingertips against my nape,
the naked skin always concealed beneath
my hair the wind blew wild. The scissors shut.
The weight fell from my shoulders to the floor.

When it was done, my father lifted me
out from the chair, and all around my feet
lay iridescent rings of gold in slants
of that late summer's blond hued afternoon.

I couldn't bear to throw them in the trash.
Instead, we tossed what burdened and what pained
us both into the night's breeze, let the bane
become a blessing to a clutch of birds.

Bluebonnets

Every Texan has a photograph like this:
bluebonnet fields, a smiling child, a sky

that's infinite. I stare down at myself
from years ago, my step-dad's cowboy hat,

my front teeth gone, my mother's rusted truck
pulled over in the grass along the highway.

But it's what happened next that I remember
most: My mom had said the flowers looked

too lovely just to leave there, south of nowhere,
to pick a few to dry them in the sun.

She was never one to follow rules,
or maybe she had never learned it's wrong,

bluebonnets aren't for picking and besides—
all the beauty in the world was made

for someone else, and it was dangerous
for our kind to just reach out and take.

I'd learned the only beauty that was mine
was me, and soon, that too, I'd give away.

But she insisted, said to bring a bunch
to lay them on the dash. I grabbed a fist

full, easy like an apple plucked from grandma's
tree back home, like opening a box

I'm not supposed to touch, or slipping secret
sweets between my lips. And nothing happens—

no sirens in the wind, no chaos seeping
from the severed roots, and just a rattler's

skin lie in the grass. I hurried back.
My mother pulled a ribbon from her hair

and tied the flowers, bluer than her eyes,
in a bouquet. She hung them upside down

and taught me every flower on the earth
belonged as much to me as anyone.

A Visit to the Aquarium at Ten

I used to swim with ankles interlocked,
pretending I was lost with the depths,

a tail as heavy as longing. This was how
I thought they spent their lives—peeking over

water, dreaming, singing songs for sailors,
hoping one would pull her from the turquoise

emptiness and make her feel complete.
So when I pressed my face against the cold

aquarium's smooth glass, I was surprised
at what I saw—a world awash with bubbles,

algae, seagrass, life. I searched for coral
hair, a glimpse of scarlet lips, a desperate

face like mine. A head of lettuce bobbed
atop the waves her coming made. She parted

water with her flippers, pebble-colored,
washed smooth with river current. Scars adorned

her back, a story of a lifetime spent
flying through the ocean over fields

of grass and sand. The head of lettuce all
but disappeared within her lips. She sang

a trill into the depths of water, called
a calf that brushed against her curves before

they disappeared into the indigo
and slate with twice the gracefulness of mermaids

in my mind. She made me long to trade
my heavy feet for flippers, join her there

within the water, learn to hold my breath,
make waves with all my mightiness and strength,

and disappear forever in the depths.

Dulce

His body wrapped in folds of black exhaust,
my father fumbles with a wrench, his head
is lost inside a pick-up's propped up hood.
I hear him curse the Texas heat. I laugh,
and tap his sunburnt shoulder, offer him
a bowl of melting ice cream. *Caramel?*
he asks, and grabs it with grease-stippled hands.
Dulce de leche, words slide off my tongue.

He asks me where I learned to talk like that.
Behind this truck, a boy with soft dark hands,
smooth tongue like caramel. But I don't say,
just shrug, breath in the heavy smell of fumes,
with melting ice cream sticky on my hands.

Prickly Pear

Like nymphs beneath the moon the women danced
to thumping beats, umbrella drinks held high.
They swayed their hips together, laughed because
they knew that men would watch them from afar
like lovesick gods and were more fun to spurn
than go home with. But Daphne, with her hair
in disarray, bare shoulders sparkling
with sweat and glitter, caught a young man's gaze—

his face was fresh, his dusty curls peeked out
from underneath a cowboy hat. He winked.
She rolled her green agave eyes, then gave
her back to him. But to his drunken eye,
in flight she was more fair. If hands like his
could snap the necks of vicious rattlesnakes,
then surely they could glide across her skin.

He slid his hand across her chest and pulled
her body close,

      My you look fancy girl,

he whispered as if as if flowers only grew
for plucking. Daphne felt her nipples bud
like rosy cacti blooms and prickly spines
emerge to meet Apollo's fingertips.

At Samson's Ford

The Samsons of today need pick-up trucks,
not lion ripping strength or holy strands
of flowing hair (for men, that's kinda queer),
suggests the salesman to my husband whose
accountant biceps hint that he could use
a little extra masculinity.

The traffic light turns red and Samson slams
the F150's brakes. The salesman, riding
shotgun at his side, sweet talks the torque,
horsepower and the sparkly rims in chrome.

A KISS song blazes from the radio,
It's "Modern Day Delilah,"

                    Same old ways.
Blondes have more fun!

                    Gene Simmons shrieks. I scoff.
The salesman peeks into the backseat, asks
how true it is—the first and only time
he speaks to me. I grasp a flaxen lock
and twirl it round my finger, might as well
just play along. He smiles, satisfied,
continues speaking in the tongues of man.

And from the corner of my eye, I see
a flash of light and search the intersection
for its sacred origin—the Texas sun
reflecting off a pair of silver bull's
balls, dangling from the truck in front of us.

The traffic light turns green and engines grunt.
I dream of scissors, songs of sharpening
a blade across a whetstone:

                    Same old ways.

If Marriage Were a Sitcom

We'd have a catchy theme song for our life
and teams of writers would define our roles—
you could play the clueless husband, me
the nagging wife. With laugh tracks, we could smile
at all our deepest insecurities—
the fear that I'll outgrow you, or you, me.
In thirty minutes, every problem's solved.
The camera would skip over all the humdrum—

nights when romance smells like bleach and dish soap
feels like just a single, tired kiss
against the nape. We'd watch our lives unfurl
in seasons, settings change but never us.
But when our story'd run its course, we'd say
we're canceled, shrug our shoulders and move on.

Love Story

If this is not a tale of love, then why
do all the pieces seem to fit? You're lying

underneath my jacked-up car, a cat
is slumbering at your side and soaking up

a tiny slant of winter's sun. You say
we must be meant for one another, joke

that each creator's made for a destroyer,
me, the one with worn out tires, drips

of dusky oil, maker of the grease-stains
on your hands. I laugh. The cat's eyes widen,

then lantanas rustle with her coming.
Half a whole, you say that I'd be broken

without you, and I ask you what your hands
would look like: idle, hungry, always clean.

The cat emerges from the overgrowth,
a mouse's body tucked into her maw

so perfectly it's almost beautiful—
a lifeless tail hanging from her lips.

Morning Commute

I taste the bitter coffee on my tongue.
It fills my throat with lukewarm hope of waking,
that somehow this will bring me back
to life. Each morning smells like gasoline,
like fumes. The sea's of pavement, reaching past
the point of vanishing. Horns cry. Engines
hum. They drown the cooing of a mourning
dove that perches on a power line,
her song foretells the sun, its resurrection
over the horizon, its warmth against
my face like breath, its rays that flood my eyes.
I pull the shade down, slip sunglasses on.

Eve Finally Makes Adam a Sandwich

My Adam was a man of simple tastes,
both at the kitchen table and in bed—
baloney with a slice of cheddar cheese,
a beer in hand, and he was satisfied.

The same routine would play out everyday:
he'd slap the meat and cheese on plain white bread
then scarf it down, get back to work outside,
as if his food were just for sustenance

and not for pleasure. One day I surprised
him in kitchen, sliced a focaccia roll
in two, slathering each piece with brie,
softened to velvet by the sun. I stacked
the meats, curled them into one another,
a blushing slice of ham, an ivory sliver
of turkey, a piece of roast beef soaked
in cabernet. And in the center, I slipped
something special in for him to try—

a gala slice so thin that when you held
it to the window, the sun shone through
like something sacred. I served him with my hands,
and smiled, nodding, knowing it was good.

Goddess on a Lonely Texas Highway

Tonight I hit a javalina dead,
not with your arrow but my Beetle's bumper.
He's lying on the shoulder, past the throes
of death, the bristles on his back erect
like spears. It's dark. My headlights and the stars
illuminate this scene—the endless brush,
barbed wire, thick brambles, prickly pear, the flames
of oilfields off into the distance, rusted
highway sign that says the nearest town's
one hundred miles away. Orion points
the way back home. Get in your car, he seems
to say, and drive like hell away from here,
no woman's land, the spaces in between;
you don't belong. My breath is shallow now.
I taste the fumes, the musk, the sorry blood
and iron in my mouth.

      Unearthly rumble,
flash of golden light. A cloud of dust
kicks up. Cicadas sing so loud they drown
the clicking of his boots against the gravel.

Returning Home

The road trip lasted longer than your body
could take and every smell reminded you
that you weren't home, the scents of lime tree blossoms,
coriander, standing water filled
the air. You ached from sitting in a car,
the radio had turned to fuzz three hours
ago outside of Monterrey, and sweat
was dripping down your legs, the summer heat
reflecting off caliche in your face.

The Rio Grande marks the final leg
of your journey. It takes five men to heave the ferry
across the slip of river into Texas;
they tug the cables, muscling you home.
Music blares—accordions and gritos.

This ride costs more than you remember, more
than just a coin slipped in between the lips
of the dying, but all you think about is home,
opening your door, unburdening
yourself of everything, a tired sigh,
and falling in your own bed, clean, cold sheets
against your skin. You paid the fare because
the body wanted nothing more than this.

You stare across the river at the trees—
the ebonies lean tired and mesquites
weep into the flowing, beryl waters.

The Funeral

No one could stop the April breeze today
from animating her hair, the pinned back curls
of his daughter as she hurried into church.
As family shuffled in, heels clicked against
the tiles like steady heartbeats, his blood flowed,
his name alive on tongues. The clocks ticked on
and cell phones rang muffled in purses as prayers
were whispered and mouthed. The songs
of reuniting filled the pews, and children's laughter
echoed, dug out nascent smiles. The flowers bloomed
white around the silent ashes, but never
did I feel more alive than when I held
his daughter's hands in mine, her eyes ablaze
with strength. I whispered my condolences.

The Grapevine

Every story is the same—there's life,
there's death, then life again, and now it's spring—
the season where my husband tends his grapevine,
runs the newest tendrils through the fingers
of one hand and holds his pruning sheers
within the other. Green is everywhere—
the canopy, the stems, the tiny buds,
but most of all, the leaves, the size of palms
and fingers reaching out in offering.

These rustling limbs are shelter for the weary:
ladybugs that come like beggars, always
hungry, fireflies that need some respite
from the sun and wait for night to dawn,
to cover up their faces, set them free,
and me, who comes in curiosity.

His clippers shush the choir of kisskadees;
the thumping of a branch against the earth
resounds across the yard and takes my breath.
He snaps the branches to a naked trunk,
a lifeless shell of what it used to be.

It's what you have to do,

                        he says, once done,
and turns the garden hose on when I ask,

If you want this water turned to wine.

Woman, Alone

It was the slice of sunshine at her back,
the evanescent whisperings of dreams

that made her rise to face another day,
cold tile against the soles of naked feet.

It was the shower's whir, the water's touch
the heat of mist like breath against the nape

that made her open up the shower curtain,
rush of chilly air on goose bumped skin.

The warmth of coffee sliding down the throat,
the maker's final moan as it clicks off,

an echoing of footsteps, then the silence.
The latch's clank, the smell of sun-washed morning

when she opens her front door, steps out
into the world to try again, alone—

a push against her back's small like a hand
ushering her out into the sun.

The Bull Rider

In Texas towns the tongues of men all taste
the same, like sour whiskey, dust between
the teeth. I think of this as neon lights
flicker above, my elbows on the bar.
A man sits down beside me, smells of sweat
and oil fields. He tucks his hands inside
his pockets, tells his story: he was once
a god on astroturf. I've heard it all
before, another song with steel guitar.
I lean in close and whisper in his ear:

I wanna to ride a god right out this town.

He nods his head as though he understands.
I rise up from my stool and walk across
the boot scuffed floor. I mount the metal bull
that only drunken tourists ever try.
My fingers wrapped around the plastic horn,

I wave goodbye to his Aegean eyes;
the smell of smoke gives way to Padre breeze.
I kick my heels off, touch my naked toes
to froth. The metal bull between my legs
turns into flesh; the Coastal Bend recedes.

We ride all night to Crete, and I become
a woman even gods cannot resist.

www.ingramcontent.com/pod-product-compliance
Lightning Source LLC
Chambersburg PA
CBHW020943090426
42736CB00010B/1248